From

FRACTALS &

CERTAIN CIRCLES

A Collection of Bad Poetry, Doggerel, and Other
Abandoned Thoughts

RC Atchisson

Printed in the United States of America
ISBN-10: 0-9974144-2-1
ISBN-13: 978-0-9974144-2-4

Library of Congress Control Number: 2016905524

Stingy Brim LLC
St. Louis, MO 63123
stingybrimllc@rcatchisson.com
www.rcatchisson.com

Cover Design by Jessica Sturgeon

This is a work of fiction. Names, characters, businesses, places, events and incidents are either the products of the author's imagination or used in a fictitious manner. Any resemblance to actual persons, living or dead, or actual events is purely coincidental.

For anyone who ever put pen to paper
to
express,
explore,
or exorcise
an emotion

and

For any and all of those
who were the inspiration
for each drop
of ink they used
in the process...

From
FRACTALS

Fractals

I woke up...late
I tried to shower
But the hot water was gone

I wanted to have toast
But there was no bread

I made the bus in time
But left all my change at home

At work...
The fax ate my memo
The copier broke
The PC went off line
My "Out" basket was empty
My "In" basket was full
And the boss said
               "Reorganization happens...
                       Budget, you know?"

The train from the city was late
The seats were full, the hand straps broke

Dinner was burned
And the cable was out

So I turned out the lights
And turned in for bed

I woke up...late

Oreos

When I was three
I looked up to Mommy and Daddy
They had the answers to all my questions
        Who is God?
        Why is the sky blue?
        How come I only have
        one birthday every year?

When I was eight
I looked up to Mom and Dad
Because they were always there when I got home
        How was your day?
        Did you learn something new?
        Do you want some Oreos?

When I was seventeen
I looked up to the folks
Because they said all the right things
        Take the car
        She's cute alright
        Here's a few extra bucks

When I was twenty one
I looked up to my parents
Because they gave me what they could
And sometimes what they couldn't
        You need the new car
        Take the last sandwich
        Don't worry; we'll take care of you

Now I look up to Bonnie and Dave
Because we are all
In the same boat
        We work

Pay bills
Get the Job Done
And sometimes, just sometimes,
enjoy some free time.

And you know what?
Every once in awhile
They still sit me down
With a big plate of Oreos
And explain why the sky is so blue...

River – Friend

The clear, blue waters
Sparkle as they roll
Over the gravel and stone
Rounding the jagged edges
And making the coarse crystals smooth.

Like the cascading streams
Firmly gliding across the elements,
You smooth my rough surfaces
And, with care, gently caress
Even the most jagged edges on me.

Daydream

You look ahead, unblinking
With a fixed stare
At words and numbers
Used to punctuate and illustrate
But do you see?

Or do you, like I,
See in your mind's eye
The two of us together
Elsewhere, anywhere in
Other times, other places?

Could we both secretly share
Those memories yet to happen
And tender moments yet to be
Of a love not yet acknowledged
By one or both?

Perfect

Funny
But perfect takes many forms.

In a dive,
No splash.

In a day,
No clouds.

In a friend,
Understanding.

In a child,
God's smile.

In a word,
You

Between the Lines

"Maybe we should just forget everything"
  (Please don't take me seriously.)

"Maybe so."
  (No chance.)

"Fine. Then I don't ever want to see you again."
  (Call me tonight.)

"Suits me just fine."
  (I'll call you tonight.)

She stares coldly.
  (You better.)

He returns the glare.
  (I promise I will)

"I hate you. I hate you! I HATE YOU!"
  (I love you.)

"I know."
  (I know.)

Vow

One
Without beginning
Without end
Forever
And always

I give to you
Golden perfection

Eternity in one hand
Love in the other
I stare into
The eyes of my future

Come share all my tomorrows

Gaze

Gaze
But not too long.
The more you look
The less there is to see.

Listen
But not too intently.
The more you hear
The crueler the words seem to sound.

Touch
But softly.
The skin you feel
May burn, freeze, or tear.

Love
But not too closely...
Distance is the only true
Measure of
Love.

Distance

I can't see the flowers
For the garden
And I can't see the smile
Behind the joke
And if my prize is waiting
'Round the corner
I know I'll never find it
Through the smoke.

I can't hear the voice
Above the chorus
And I can't find my tunnel
With its light
And if a cloud waits
With a silver lining
It's camouflaged and slips by
At midnight.

I've got to put some distance
Between me and who I am
I've got to put together a better
Version of this man
I need to make a resolution
To see things as they really are
And watch them from a distance
But, in the end, one not too far.

I don't get the hoof beats
Just the stampede
I can't see reflections
Just a hall of mirrors
My house of cards is built
On these illusions
A stillborn, silent voice
Is always near

A captive to the trappings that surround me
A prisoner to the maze
That is my mind
No price, no peace, no block of cheese
Help me back on track now please
Some new dilemmas
I'll be sure to find

I've got to put some distance
Between who I was and am
I've got to redefine
This latest version of the man
Need to let some time accumulate
Let the miles behind me grow
And maybe someday I'll begin to like
The man I begin to know...

Unfinished Verse

Poems are never finished
Just abandoned.

So, too, are you
For now.

Though I look
To directions far

Away from the love
That was you,

Know that I still
Think of yesterday's hopes

And tomorrow's dreams;
Memories yet to happen.

But
For now
I leave behind
The rhyme and verse
I call my favorite poem —
You.

Rope

From that tree
      She tied the rope.

Her life, she thought,
      Required some pruning.

Seasons change, people change
She carefully tied knots.
Meticulous,
Calculated,
Tight.

Leaves fall from trees
Suspended in the air for a time
Floating.
So would she.

But leaves abruptly land as well
Left to die,
Rot.
She would not.

And so, at the end of her rope,
She tied a knot and held on.

New Game

I can't.
No, I don't want.
No, I can
And I wouldn't mind
If I was better at it.
Never mind
I just want to play a new game.

You

You
My love
My life
My muse
Of unspoken
Inspiration
Millions of dreams
Locked in your eyes
Help me to see
Tomorrow
And make me
Want to be there
With
You

Silence

When silence passes
She shakes a cold chill
That grabs at her shoulders
As she watches the procession
File into the yard of resting souls.

When Silence passes
She shakes her head
At a tragedy halfway
Around the world, fights a tear
And turns the channel.

When silence passes
She watches the horrified faces
Of onlookers who stare at
The wreckage and wonder if
They suffered or went quickly.

When she passes Silence
She looks ahead with the memory of
A chill, the world, the horrified faces
And she smiles because again
She has looked past Silence.

Timing

You roll the stop sign by Pizza Hut
...The very day a cop pulls in to try
       Their new lunch buffet...

You realize football games, road trips,
And late nights have eaten up all your
Legitimate sick days
...Only to come down with
       Chicken pox...

The boss stops by your desk
...To discover you doing cross-words
With his anniversary pen you picked up
From someone else's desk...

Okay, sure, you thought you were just borrowing
A pen from someone in accounting...
Who knew...?

You show her your old phone book to prove
That it's empty
...Only to discover a number long-forgotten
       And, you though, long-gone.

Same difference
Timing is timing
Bad timing is endless
And merciless
And as regular...
As clockwork.

Give It Wings

Sometimes when you look my way
I know that you see
Shadows of another life,
Of who I used to be.
But that was a time,
Before you came along.
Now it seems that any time
Without you must be wrong.

Still sometimes I wonder
Just how tightly you'll hold.
If you cover a fire,
Soon the embers grow cold.
All I ask is your trust.
Let me know that you care,
And believe that when you turn
To see me I'll be there.

Let me have your love,
Give it wings.
Then let it carry us
To better things.
Just hold me close,
But let me learn how to fly.
And I'll always come home to you
By and by.

It's a world full of strangers,
And we've so much to do
That by the end of the day,
I need to be with you.
But in between times,
When I'm alone,
I'd like to discover some things on my own.

And when I'm finished seeing
What there is to see,
Just know that I want you
To be holding me.

So let me have your love,
Give it wings.
Then let it carry us
To better things.

Just hold me close
But let me learn to fly,
And I'll always come home —
To you
By and by...

Sunday Mourning

The ringing echoes
Through empty halls.
I sit against
A bare wall
Debating the merits
Of answering.
When, at last,
I do
I discover that
The voice belongs
To you.
And suddenly
The rooms fill
Once again.

Your jacket drapes
Itself on the stairway.
Your bike
Clutters
The hall.
School books and magazines
Bury the coffee table
And your CDs
Fill the air with
Songs I once complained about.
Our pictures redecorate the walls
As posters, paintings, and more
Once again adorn the whiteness.

But when you have finished saying
What you have to say...
A click,
A silence,
A dial tone...

And the rooms again are empty,
So, I sit against
A bare wall.

Reflections

The cold water gently receives
A warm body.

Praying for answers to questions eternal
Awaiting an epiphany of meaning
Anticipating a baptism of renewed hope.

As he stares into the pond,
Each clear vision
Of a figure
Mired in the mud we never see
Is disrupted
By ripples from each
Twist, turn breath, heartbeat
Thought.
A new image is set only to be erased
Again.
This pattern – turbulence, peace
Continues as he
Walks
Deeper and deeper,
Slower
And slower
Eyes always affixed
Just inches
Before him on the image
The water sends in return.

"Are these the legs that carried me
Through the darkest tunnels of my life?"
The water breaks.

"Are these the arms and muscles that once held
The ideals and dreams of youth?"
The water moves.

"Are these the shoulders that so often
Acted as a brace for others in their sorrow?"
The water swallows deeper.

"Are these the eyes of a man
Who sees no other way?"

Driftwood

In a sea of emotion
                    I cling to you

Fighting an undertow of uncertainty
                            I embrace you

I guess the occasional splinter is necessary
                            For the constant support

You give me reason to fight the tide
                            I give you reason to be

We are
                    For the time
                                    Inseparable

Tomorrow's Voice

Sometimes I'd stop and wonder
"Who am I today?
Do I say the things I think?
Do I think the things I say?"
So much time has passed me by
Time I never really owned
At times I feared my only hope
Was to run and be alone
In seclusion
One finds silence
In silence one finds peace
And with peace even my deepest fears
Could momentarily release
My broken heart and broken spirit
From their grasp and let them be
But instead I'd drown myself
In a sea of miseries –
Dark images and shadows
A past I could not escape,
A life I wore like battle scars
Pulling punches that I'd take
I wanted what I wanted
Took what they would give
Sometimes more if they would let me
Never living, I'd just live
Then one day I heard a whisper
That echoed like a shout
In a soul empty and lonely
Now my heart tried calling out
Realized I couldn't answer
I thought "What more could I say?"
So I pulled my weary head
From its pillow one more day
And that's how I took it
Hours, daily, scene by scene,

Over chaos came new whispers
What did the message mean?
I stopped listening, started hearing
Let go, guided by my heart
Felt miles go by and years just die
Found me right back at the start
I looked down a road I'd travelled
Swore I'd do it right this time
Guided by some inspiration
An unseen hand now tugged at mine
So I followed without watching
Learned to take a leap of faith
Till I released the hand that guided
Blindly drifting my own way
Without direction, inspiration,
Or the hope to carry on
I unearthed a box I'd buried
Found those memories I thought gone
They dusted off their scabbards
Drew their swords for battles more
I dropped to my knees in silence
To lose a war I'd lost before.
Till once again the voice said "Let go
Drop your weapons, live, be free"
Then I saw the swords start falling
From hands that belonged to me
Saw the ground shatter my sorrows
Saw them fade again to dust
Far too weak to face this new world
That soft voice whispered "You must"
Once again the hand that guided
Gently set me in my place
It touched my heart, dusted my shoulders,
And wiped the tears from my cold face
As it did I searched the heavens
To find the sun resting above
Through my tears I saw a rainbow

The voice called that spectrum love
Now each day I look at bravely
I've learned to savor every choice
And when I'm lost in darkness
I listen for tomorrow's voice.

Vision

I was a child who saw the world
Through Technicolor glasses.
Everything was larger and louder than
It should have been.
As I grew, I outgrew the spectrum specs
And settled on opaque shades.
Life somehow seems more romantic
Through Wayfarers.
As muscles weaken
Bifocals will become necessary
And, ultimately, useless.
Then, no lens can show me
What I need to see
And the picture
Will only be apparent
In my mind's eye.

Grace

The parish rests easy
As the old church bells ring.
Families huddle at dinner,
Harvests God's blessing brings.

Giving thanks for the family
Except Eddie, they think,
"Who wouldn't buy me a bottle
For my afternoon drink."

"And Roland, a nice boy
But a little too gay.
Perhaps he and his 'friend'
Should live some other way."

And not Louise, they then mention,
"She was the first to point out
That the money from Mom's will
Was handled strangely, no doubt."

For friends and for leaders
They also said grace
Except for that Lois Flanders,
"You know she's just so two-faced."

And the Mitchells whose dog
"Runs without any leash"
And their painted up daughter,
"A puppy in heat."

"Oh and don't bless Father Tinker
Whose school we support,
Raised tuition a dollar __
Why he's just the sort!"

So on run exceptions
As to God they them told.
Till at last both their dinners
And their hearts grew stone cold.

Conversation

Breakfast was always
Cold by the time
He sat down
But the conversation was good.
She spoke of work,
Mom, and Oprah
As he nodded intently
Offering smiles of encouragement
And silent support.

On the bus
Familiar faces
Struggled for seating
But the conversation
Was good.
They rambled of jobs,
Sports, and politics
While he nodded politely
Sharing only raised eyebrows
And feigned understanding.

At coffee breaks
Worker bees swarmed
To the caffeine
But the conversation
Was good.
They talked about raises
And reorganizations
As he nodded gravely
Implying his interest and
Mutual thought.

At the funeral
Everyone stood by
His coffin

But the conversation was good.
They spoke of streets,
Bodies, and unlocked open windows
While he, in their presence, said
Nothing
As he had so often before.

They told of their long and in-depth
Conversations
With the man they all
Thought they knew so well.
He never mentioned a problem
They firmly agreed
Never once in the many
Times that they talked.

And so they went on
This circle of strangers:
A wife
Passengers
And stunned worker bees
Chatting incessantly
With relative ease
Of people and things they knew
Little about.

And despite the occasion
And their own lack of knowledge
The conversation was good.

Understood

The first words that you said to me
I could cite them chapter and verse.
The first smile that you shared
I could spend countless hours describing.
The girl I knew and the woman I know
I could talk about for days at a time.
And the hopes inspired of thinking of her
Have penned a thousand lines.
But the truth of the matter
Is that of all my musings, ramblings
And recollections,
The most important words
Have gone unsaid
Unspoken
Understood

Cascade

The pictures and the paintings
On my tapestry of time
Are all a stitch from fading
As my hard work all unwinds.

And my common threads aren't shared
By the weavers anymore,
And they don't fit the needles
Quite as well as once before.

So I watch the frayed edge give way
To spools as they unwind
And watch my life's work come undone
In cascading frames of time.

Sunlight

Like Icarus I see the sun
But not part of the sky
The light he seeks shines up above
And mine glows in your eyes.
Still a clear and present danger
Sends him tumbling back to ground
And no more safe am I to touch
This love that I have found.

My wings are made of memories
No stronger than his paraffin
And foolish pride, like him,
May send me far from where I've been.
Far from the security
The safety of my home
Aloft into the azure winds
To search for you alone.

And from the earth mere mortals wish
To reach forbidden heights
While all I wish is for an end
To all my lonely nights.
So I will brave uncharted land
To this new course stay true
And I will shadow mountains high
If awaiting me are you.

The land below can't anchor me
Love lifts me to the skies
And even on my darkest days
I'll still find sunlight in your eyes.

Stolen Glances

Anticipating stolen glances
Or a moment of our own
I devour perfumed letters
Sit for hours by the phone.
Miles away and worlds apart
We lead our separate lives,
And once we make connections
We're always seconds from "goodbye".
So we make our plans in private
Try to talk of nothing much
While we hold our breath imagining
A secret, tender touch.
Forced to steal our time together,
Time that's stolen in return,
We stare into the fire
To find that stolen glances burn.

The Garden

She wanted a garden
She firmly decided
One to decorate
Rooms in her life

So
From a garden
Rich in prospects
She gently
Culled her bouquet

Each unique
Unto himself
Varied
In color,
Origin,
And fragrance

With excited hands
She would
Pull them
One by one
From the safety
Of their ground
Holding them
Briefly
And setting them
Aside
Just in case...

One bloom
In particular
Caught her attention
It was simple
Unrefined

And wild
He appeared
Common to
Everyone but
Her
Somehow
She found a
Natural beauty
In him

So She
Lovingly
And cautiously
Pulled him
To her
He was by far
Her favorite bloom

With darting eyes
She smiled
As new blossoms
Seemed to promise more
So she grabbed
And pulled
And held
And cast aside
Until she had
All but emptied
The garden

When finally satisfied
She had found
The flower of her choice
She returned to find
It among the many
Others she had
Plucked

Before and after

Till at last she found him
Thirsty and dying
From lack of care
And despite
The attempts her eyes made
To water it
Her favorite bloom
Long ignored and
All but lost
Among the sea of petals

Faded

Between the Lines '94

"Hi, Honey."
(Why are you home so early?)

"Hi, Sweetheart."
(Why do you look so surprised?)

"How was your day?"
(Are you staying?)

"Long."
(Sorry, tonight *you* go out.)

"Well, then just relax tonight."
(I'll call him.)

"I know.
(I know.)

Going out with the girls?"
(Going out with him?)

"Uh-huh."
(Yes.)

"Have fun."
(What changed?)

"I will."
(We did.)

"Be good."
(Goodbye.)

"Thanks."
(Goodbye.)

And Your Eyes

I listened
To the raindrops
And imagined
Them as tears
And your eyes
Cried them.
The light flashed
In the midnight air
Bookending scattered
Memories of
Whispers,
Words,
And your eyes.
So I wandered
Aimlessly in
The hallow of me
Looking for that
Which I'd lost,
Your heart's
Warmth
And your eyes'
Invitation,
That gaze that
Could draw me in
And keep me for
Hours
Even if only in memory.
And your eyes
Always seemed to
Hold the answers
To all my
Questions.
They could caress,
Understand,
Accept,

And love
But tonight
I drive
Without your
Touch
And without your understanding
And probably without your love
Realizing that the two places
I find myself
Most lost are
In the midnight air
And your eyes.

Our Beach

Our beach could be
A dream
Untouched
Where we'll walk
Savoring the delight
Of sand
Under foot.

Our beach could be
A tapestry
Unwound
Whose landscape
Weaves a fortress
Of hope
Against
The Undertow.

Our beach could be
A canvass
Unpainted
Where tomorrow waits
For us
And plays
Patiently.

Our beach could be
The common ground
Where we'll rediscover
Ourselves and
Each other

Where we will stop
To watch
A sun set on
Our footprints

Closing the door on
Yesterday

Where we will awake
To watch
A sun rise on
Untouched sand
Opening a window for
The future

Our beach could be
Any or all
Of these things.
So it sits
Sculpted
By time's tide
Waiting to be
Walked,
Woven, and
Painted

But, for now,
Our beach is just
A dream.

Unopened Letters

The envelopes still
Look as fresh
As the day they arrived
Postmarked
Days on end
From the same
Point of origin
Awaiting a reply that
Will never come.
They sit.

He wonders when he sees
His collection
Because
In this condition
They are powerful,
Much more so
Than the words
Contained inside
The unbroken seals could ever be.

They might be declarations of love
Promising days
Of memories still to come
Or
Pleadings of forgiveness
Asking for another
Chance to make things
Right.

Perhaps they hold harsh
Words scribbled in anger
Over a misplaced thought
Or ill-chosen word
Or

Maybe a simple
"Hello, I miss you."

He doesn't care.
Not anymore

Now, it all really
Just depends on
His mood,
And he can
Adjust accordingly.

So he simply
Runs a still gentle
Fingertip over the
Return address
Of each new addition and
Discovers and rediscovers
Moment by moment and
Unopened letter by
Unopened letter
How he feels
Today.

Because, sometimes
Some things are best left
Undisturbed
Some questions best
Unanswered
And some letters
Unopened.

Perhaps

Perhaps
It was the evening air
      the music, or the drink
But a glance had left me reeling
Time and self fell out of synch.
Through a teeming crowd I found a face
      that pulled me from my home
Amidst the crowd, the song, the lights
Stood just we two alone.
When the conversation ended
She smiled and turned her head
I hoped we'd talk again this way.
"Perhaps" was all she said.

Days, not weeks, soon after
We began our waltz with words
No dreams remained untouched, unsaid
No sentiment unheard.
Volumes passed between us
Sharing hopes and fears and more
At the threshold of the future
Standing just outside its door.
Often I would wonder
Aloud or in my head
Will we ever share tomorrow?
"Perhaps" is all she said.

Time can be an ally
Often patience is a friend
It took some miles and months before
I saw her once again.
When I did my world was different
She spoke of years and growing old
Together with a family
Braving torrents, rain, and cold.

She said we'd celebrate the sunshine
On life's riches we'd be fed.
I wondered if she meant those words.
"Perhaps," was all she said.

I woke to find a letter
On paper I had seen before.
It told of what she needed
"This," she said, "but more."
She wrote of beaches, sand, and sunsets
And a girl that she once knew
She was journeying to find her
Not a passage, though, for two.
"You are my heart, my soul, my mind"
Is how the letter read.
"Will the fates bind us together?
Perhaps," is all it said.

The phone call came by accident
Meant for another friend
She'd been sick some time they said
This seemed to be the end.
Standing there beside her
As I always knew I'd be
I remembered all our moments
When she looked up and smiled at me
"I didn't leave for me," she said
"I couldn't say 'Goodbye' this way."
She spoke of scorpions and frogs and such
Explaining nature's way.

Sometimes one doesn't plan to
But still finds another soul
That for reasons we can't understand
Somehow makes us whole.
And I knew what she was trying
In her own words to get through.

I just smiled and held her to me
And whispered that I loved her too.

Through tears I watched her fading
As I gently stroked her head
"I'll see you on the other side," I smiled
"I know," was all she said.

Didn't We

We didn't have a lot of time
So we didn't waste a bit.
We couldn't comprehend goodbye
So we didn't think of it.

And you didn't make a promise
But the things you didn't say
Didn't stay my soaring hopes and dreams
Or make them fade away.

You didn't want to talk about
Questions best unasked
And you didn't hesitate to say
This moment, too, could pass.

But I didn't listen closely
To words I didn't want to hear.
And it didn't seem to matter
What we side-stepped was so near.

We didn't say the simple things
That others say too much.
Words tossed about too carelessly
Cease to mean or touch.

We offered other, lesser words
That didn't share as well
The things we didn't need to say,
Things we could simply tell.

So we danced around the issue
Pretending not to see
And managed to still somehow say
What we didn't.
Didn't we?

Watered Down

The reflection, to him, always
Seems so much happier
A stranger to the problems
That live outside the glass.

His lips split
The mirror
Like a
Lover
Drinking of her
Slowly
Longingly
Lastingly
Losing himself
In her kiss,
After each and
Every embrace
The reflection
Smiles more broadly
And he caresses his love
More gently
Explaining himself
Time and again
Till at last
Both the
Lover and
Reflection
Are gone.

And he sits alone
Once again
A stranger
Outside the glass.

Shakespeare's Pages

Between Shakespeare's pages
You'll find the source of my emotion
The flint for the spark that set
My whole world into motion.
It's pressed there, but still as sweet
As when you laid it in my hand
A fragile beauty so delicate
A floral castle not unlike sand.

I think back to the night
I hear the music in the air
I see the smile dance in your eyes
And the flower in your hair.
From the moment you left
I searched for traces of you here
But all I had were my memories
And a dying souvenir.

So between Shakespeare's pages
I placed the petals with affection
From time to time I stop to visit them
Perhaps more truthfully, correction,
I come to offer up across the miles
My soul and restless heart
Or the little bit that's left with me
Now you hold the largest part.

When I need inspiration
I walk the garden in my book
And in my mind's most private eyes
It's together that we look
Upon this seed we have planted
Among the words, the text, and then
We stand beside one another
As the blossom blooms again.

Between Shakespeare's pages
Our bouquet begins to rise
I hear the music in the air
I see the smile dance in your eyes
Watching what we have nurtured
Maybe moments, maybe ages
Sharing love inside this garden that began
In Shakespeare's pages.

Moments

It only takes a second
To connect.
The surge of excitement
The adrenaline rush
The impulse
The moment.

It takes a moment
To change your world.
The right words
The sly smile
The memory of
Moments yet to happen.

It takes a minute
To gather yourself
To think
To dream
To reach out.

In a heartbeat
Everything changes.
Someone walks
In a door you've opened
And you want to
Keep them there
Forever.

It takes a miracle
For them to stay.
The door swings
Both ways
And time is a bandit
Stealing your

Seconds
Minutes
Moments
And miracles.
Until all you are left with
Are heartbeats...
And in a heartbeat
Everything changes.

Acceleration

Acceleration
Sends the body
Into shaking fits.
Each new twist
And turn
Forces your wheels
To hug the road
For a fleeting
Sensation of security
A straightaway invites
More speed as
You shift into high gear
Both passenger and driver
Locked in for the ride.
Ignoring flashing reds
They look at one another
And convince themselves that
The signal was green.
A glance past the windshield
At the outside world
Warrants a rapid change of course...
Obstacles.
Now the ride seems dangerous.
Once smooth blacktop
Has turned to
Unfinished gravel
And dirt.
Suspension is rocked
And stability tested.
Ability,
Nerve,
And judgment
Are called and recalled
Into question

By both.
Up ahead
A steady green
Gives them pause
As they hit the brakes.
At the same instant
Another car careens
Through the intersection
On red
Its passengers
Looking at one another
Convinced that the signal was
Green.

The Catch

Fishermen
And fishers of men
Repeatedly troll
The sea of human faces
Searching for the other fish
We've heard so much of.
Our few catches are discarded —
Too small. Wrong type.
Not the right time.
While our nets drag...
Sometimes in water too shallow for our own good.
And others in troubled waters, still at the surface.
We pilot our lonely vessels
Through fair weather and storms
In search of it.
When our efforts finally
Snare an oyster
Small, dark, and secretive,
We admire our feat
But resist opening our prize
For fear of what we'll find.
Will it be the pearl
For which we have so long looked
Or just an undigested bit of sand —
Misleading and insignificant
In the true scheme of our journey?
So, in cupped hands, as if a jewel,
We hold these cold, lifeless shells
That may or may not hold our tomorrow
For fear that the answer we find upon opening
May mean another day's fishing
Or, worse yet.
Dropping anchor at last.

The Lover

To a true
Lover
Of life
Everything is precious.

To them
Moments are milestones
And markers
On the grand scheme
Of life's journey.

No path goes un-walked
No song unsung
No garden untended
No seed unsown.

The lover can
Coax a bloom
From the weakest of buds
Or harvest bundles
From once fallow fields.

To a true
Lover
Of life
Each soul is precious.

For them
Life is a pageant
Of opportunities
Great and small
Chances to touch
Or be touched.

No hand is un-held
No tear left unanswered
No heart untouched
No life left unchanged.

The lover can
Spread the wings
Of those afraid to fly
And mend the faith
Of the most broken spirit.
The lover can savor raindrops
Or linger in the sunlight.
The lover
Can embrace words
Or bask in the silence.
The lover
Can settle a restless spirit
Or set it to flight.

It all depends on the moment

And to a true
Lover
Of life

The moment is everything
And everything is
Precious

Incidentally

Being incidental
Means
Being expendable.
With or
Without
You, their
Suns will set
Tides will break
Or hearts will soar.

Being incidental
Means
Always listening
For that
Other shoe to drop
Today
Tomorrow
Eventually.

Being incidental
Is always an accident.
No one
Plans
To erase
The smile
From your face
Or your heart.
It just happens.

Being incidental
Means
Being willing
To come
Or go
Freely

When they ask
When they don't
When you should.

Being incidental
Means resigning yourself
To the
Fact
That you
Are simply a
Moment in their lives.
And, incidentally,
Moments pass.

The Best That Ever Happens

If the worst that ever happens
Is I lose you for a time
And the hours in between us
Turn out of sight to out of mind.
And if the worst that ever happens
Is all my dreams then don't come true,
Then the best that ever happened
To me, is loving you.

When supper smiles are memories
And old confidences fade,
We may forget the words we used
But not the promises we made.
When I'm looking to the sky,
I'll think, "At least we share the moon."
Believe the best that ever happened
To me, is loving you.

If the curtain closes on our play
And leaves us with an empty stage,
If we close the cover of our book
Atop an empty page,
If the music ends and finds us
Dancing alone as people do,
Please know the best that ever happened
To me, is loving you.

Midnight

She took her troubles
To the midnight waters
And left the comfort of
Her life on shore
She stared into the pitch
That was her memory
To loosen shackles
She would wear no more
The ghosts that haunted her
Stayed in the shadows
Her phantoms were
Empowered by the dark
So when they made their
Stabs out at her conscience
She couldn't see them
As they hit their mark.

Enlightenment can come
From understanding
Encouragement is
Just a loving hand
That guides you through
The darkest of recesses
Looking back she smiled
At her love in the sand
She closed her eyes as
She turned toward her demons
Resolved to make a
Stranger of the night
And when she opened them
Upon the waters
She saw the shadows
In a different light.

As with shadows
They were mere illusions
Like Plato's people
On the cavern wall
In the darkness
They could rule as monarchs
But illuminated
They weren't royal at all

She returned to her
Love at the coastline
Casts her ghosts adrift
Onto the sea
Without them she would
Start to live a new life
And without her
They would simply cease to be

From time to time
She recollects that midnight
The waters where she
Put her troubles down
And though they made
Themselves known for a moment
She rose above and
They just finally drowned

Song

The world sings
To me
A new song

It is on
The wind
That breathes life
Into the hallow of me

It is on the current of
The river
Calling me to her banks

It sounds forth from
The night sky
And its tapestry of stars

It is in
The very heart
Of you

Far too long
Have I turned
A deaf ear
To this
The sweetest of
Life's music?

Turning my back
To the wind
Refusing to drink
From the current
Closing my eyes
On the constellations

But now
Your song
Fills me
With every note
Of your sweet being

And I want to sing
And listen
And it carries on the wind
And floats atop the current
And soars to the heavens

The Man I Used to Be

Watching you from the window
In the glass
I saw
A ghost
Of the man I used to be.

This familiar phantom
Had grown a bit with age.
He had grown with me.

The vague features on
His face had softened a little,
But the piercing stare had not.
Still, the man I used to be
Wore the same stony countenance
And cold stare
Showing little or no emotion,
Convincing me
Little
Or
Nothing
Had changed.

Suddenly, as you slipped in the snow
I smiled,
And I saw a remarkable thing.
The man I used to be
Smiled too.
I guess he really had grown
With me.

As you blew me a kiss
Through the crystal air and slipped again,
I laughed.
And

The man I used to be
Disappeared forever
In a warm fog of forgotten yesterdays.
And when it had cleared,
In his place stood
The man I now am

From

CERTAIN CIRCLES

Certain Circles

In certain circles
They won't discuss
Life's little uglies
The unmade bed
Spotted dishes
And moldy bread
Of their private lives

In certain circles
They won't unveil
The family photos
Where no one smiles
The bones behind
Each closed door

In certain circles
They won't acknowledge
The salacious grin
The ill-placed hand
The back room sobs and whispers

In certain circles
Families dance
Like zombies
Through a minefield
Ignoring shrapnel
Numb to pain

In certain circles
Fractured families
Travel round and round

The Chasm

The bridge of our emotion
Slowly splintered over time
Stranding us at separate ends
Your universe and mine

We both had a horizon
That kept tomorrow in our view
But no longer did you stand with me
Nor did I look with you

At the landscape of a future
Shared by lovers, shared by friends
Instead our common ground
Were separate parcels once again

You struck out for the sunlight
As I settled into dusk
While the bridge that we once traveled
Turned, boards and ropes, to dust

When you returned from twilight
To bridge the chasm of my trust
The tears I cried in caution
Caused the new girders to rust

So separately together
We walked toward each respective rise
And if again our roads rejoined
It was far beyond our eyes

In the hours since our moment
The miles between have grown
And that bridge across the chasm
Is still the sweetest I have known

Coming Home

Home is no mere address
Though it's the place where we all start
The foundation for our memories
A touchstone for our heart

Familiar sounds and voices,
For us life's sweetest song
Whose notes when once resolved
To our ears, urge us along

Home is not a feeling
It's love and attitude
A serenity that finds your soul
And washes over you

Home is in a friend's kind word
Or in a lover's smile
And though you feel you've traveled far
Home's with you all the while

Home is like a harbor safe
In storms and weather fair
And you never need to search for home
You'll know when you are there

Though coming home may simply mean
Taking another's hand
Your home is truly in the eyes of
One who says "I understand"

I'll Dream You a Poem

I'll dream you a poem
Every second of my days.
I'll make familiar fresh,
And sing old songs in new ways.
I'll make each day's adventure
A treasure you will hold
And promise that our moments
Will weigh as precious gold.
Each tear you cry I'll gather
In a bottle or a glass.
Each smile you share I'll save
For days when other rains won't pass.
When I've bottled each, and
Once we've sifted through the brine
Together we'll combine them to
Then taste life's sweetest wine.
I'll make each walk a waltz
Beneath night's diamonds high above.
Yes, I'll dream you a poem,
And I'll call that poem love.

Embrace

She comes to him
He dutifully
Welcomes her with
A smile

Beyond her shoulders
He spies
Wanting eyes
Crying out to him
From the safety
Of another ill-chosen
Embrace

He longs to
Free those eyes
Yet resigns himself
To his post
Because, he thinks,
She needs him

But beyond his shoulders
She spies
Wanting eyes...

Passage

Across a wide tomorrow
I stare into an abyss
That I've traveled in my mind before
But never quite like this

Before, it was an image
Little more than a vague dream
But each step that I take forward
Tells me "All is as it seems"

Too far gone for me to turn back
Not far enough to understand
With measured breaths I study stillness
And the contours of the land

Colors strangely vibrant
I See blend and fade to pitch
In the darkness I can feel my life
Unwinding stitch by stitch

Once inside the cavern
I'm encompassed by its chill
No blindness stays my journey
I stumble forward still

The life I led unscrambles
Makes mosaic of my past
Then, ahead, amidst the darkness
I see new shadows cast

For shadows to exist I know
That means there must be light
So through the black I battle
And toward the glow I fight

Once safely through the tunnel
In the sun I make my stand
To find the life I knew is
Now a distant, foreign land

Colors are more vibrant
Sounds are ever sweet
And at last I can now call home
The land beneath my feet

Surrender

I surrender
To the waters
To the midnight
The waves

I offer up my wants
To the night air
The heavens
A dream defiled
And much maligned

To the pitch
The somber hue
Which beckons me,
Seduces me,
Envelopes me.
I surrender...

Two Tides

For a time two tides traveled the earth
Swept 'cross the seas as one
They battled forces mighty and played
'Neath a consenting sun

Though once they both did swim alone
Now enjoined were they
Two solitary powers
Together making way

Definition faded
No longer two apart
A sole image was forming
One fluid soul and heart

They shared each up, each down, each roll
Themselves a force of one
But the world can pull unkindly
'Neath a consenting sun

Soon the tide again grew twain
Though not two like before
Each tide, this time, had taken some
And given something more

To view them with the naked eye
No changes could be seen
But each tide now shared of the other
Despite the miles between

The waves of time just carried on
Unceasing as they are
One tide craved its home shore
The other, oceans far

So slowly they did separate
These two tides wide and vast
Each embraced new waters
Yet held moments of its past

And on they did roll, both near and far
Their journeys not yet done
Holding fast to what the other gave
'Neath a consenting sun

Where Angels Fear

Where angels fear
So tread I

Into moments unwritten
Where memories wait patiently
To be sculpted
By time's artisans.

Where angels fear
So speak I

Wanting words
And songs unsung, waiting
For life to be breathed into them
By love's chorus.

Where angels fear
So reach I

Into a past, bittersweet
A present, unsettled
And a future waiting for
Its shores to be defined
By the waters of understanding
And hope.

Where angels fear
So stand I

In ground long untended
Where I pray for change
And from which
I make my declaration
Of love to the heavens...

Where angels fear
I did not hear

My answered prayer
In the sculpting
The harmony or
The definition

When She Comes

When she comes
In her own time
Of her own accord
Into my existence

Years peel away
Revealing colors
I'd long considered lost
From the palette of me

The blue in my eyes
                    sparkles
The red in my cheeks
                    blossoms
The olive in my skin
                    deepens

Reacting
        To her touch
        Her scent
        Her smile
        Her coming

When she comes
        Into my sight
        Within my reach

Beyond my comprehension

Words once frightening
And strong fail me,
Stay me, teach me
As they lose and gain meaning

Trust
      Gives itself willingly to her
Love
      Follows suit
Always
      Understands why

Growing
      Because of
      Beside
      Before
           her

When she comes
      To take my hand
      To steal my breath
      To touch my heart

Time loses
All sense of self
As she turns its facets
One upon the other

Yesterday
      Wishes it were
           Today with her
Today
Longs to be
      Tomorrow
           By her side

Now
        Envies Forever

Understanding at once
Everything changes
Everything brightens
Everything grows
Where and
When she comes

Nantucket Red

I take to the skies above her
Through the night, atop her sound
Aloft I part the moonlit clouds
She lies waiting on the ground

Beyond me only darkness
Ships below send waves to break
I jettison my sorrows
And they're swallowed by the wake

Of those off to see my lady
My love, my life, my home.
In moments they'll alight her
As I depart alone

So until once more together
Her treasures now abed
I bid farewell my Lady Grey
And dream Nantucket Red